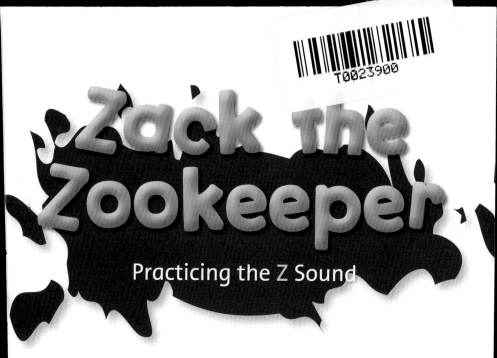

Zack the Zookeeper

Practicing the Z Sound

Serena Snyder

Rosen
Classroom™

Zack is a zookeeper.

Zack works at the zoo.
Zack loves zoo animals!

Zack feeds the lizards.

Lizards can be lazy.
Lizards live in the desert.

Zack feeds the zebras.

The zebras are noisy.

Zack likes zebras the best.
There are a dozen zebras.

Zebras can zoom around.
Zebras are fast!

Zorro is the best zebra!
Zack gives Zorro treats.

Zorro loves Zack, too.

Zack is a great zookeeper!
Zack loves to work at the zoo.